This
fun activity book
belongs to:

_____

Melo and Friends Activity Book

Copyright © 2022 by Christian Art Kids, an imprint of Christian Art Publishers,
PO Box 1599, Vereeniging, 1930, RSA

© 2022
First edition 2022

Based on *Melo's Kingdom* by Thuli Madonsela with Wenzile, Khulekile and Zedekiah Msimanga

Cover designed by Christian Art Kids
Designed by Christian Art Kids
Images used under license from Shutterstock.com

Scripture quotations are taken from the Contemporary English Version © 1991, 1992, 1995 by American Bible Society. Used by permission.

Scripture quotations are taken from the New Century Version®. Copyright © 2005 by Thomas Nelson. Used by permission. All rights reserved.

Scripture quotations are taken from the *Holy Bible*, New International Version®, NIV® Copyright © 1973, 1978, 1984, 2011 by Biblica, Inc.® Used by permission. All rights reserved worldwide.

Scripture quotations are taken from the *Holy Bible*, New Living Translation, copyright © 1996, 2004, 2015 by Tyndale House Foundation. Used by permission of Tyndale House Publishers, Carol Stream, Illinois 60188. All rights reserved.

Scripture quotations are taken from The Message, copyright © 1993, 1994, 1995, 1996, 2000, 2001, 2002 by Eugene H. Peterson. Used by permission of NavPress. All rights reserved.

Printed in China

ISBN 978-1-77637-046-7

© All rights reserved. No part of this book may be reproduced in any form without permission in writing from the publisher, except in the case of brief quotations in critical articles or reviews.

22 23 24 25 26 27 28 29 30 31 – 10 9 8 7 6 5 4 3 2 1

Printed in Shenzhen, China
OCTOBER 2021
Print Run: PUR401924

MELO & FRIENDS ACTIVITY BOOK

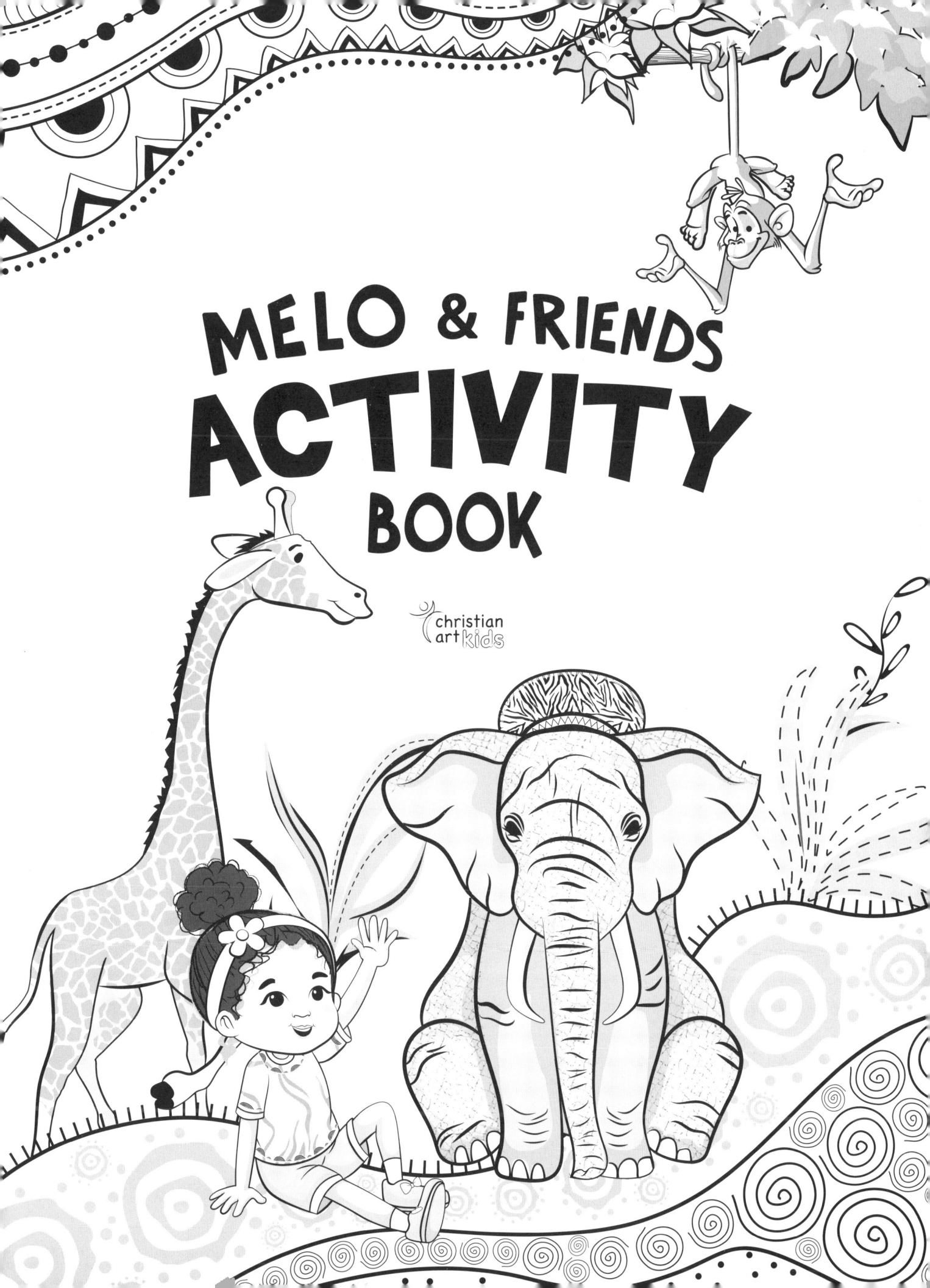

christian art kids

MEET MELO AND HER FRIENDS

Color the pictures of Melo's animal friends.

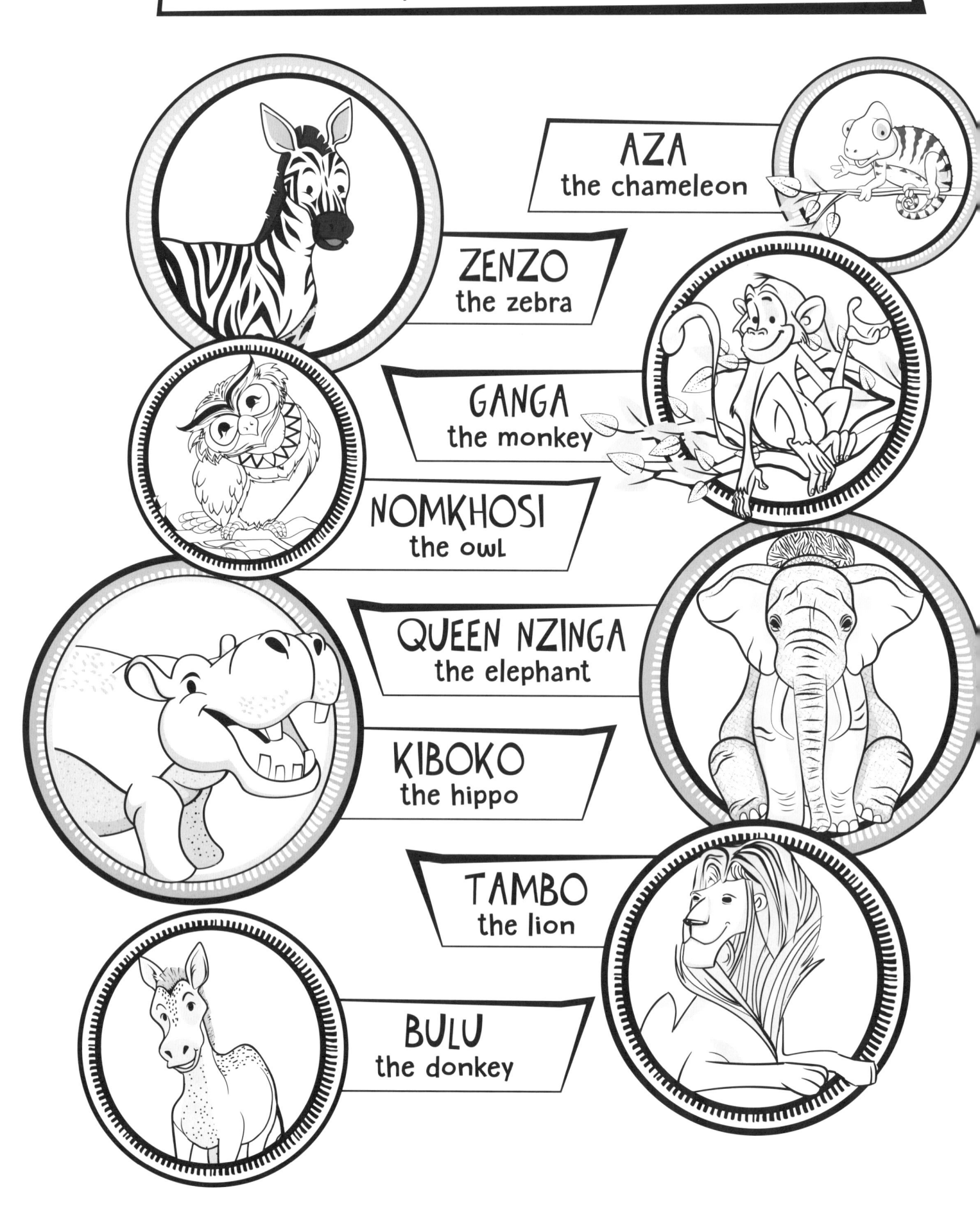

AZA
the chameleon

ZENZO
the zebra

GANGA
the monkey

NOMKHOSI
the owl

QUEEN NZINGA
the elephant

KIBOKO
the hippo

TAMBO
the lion

BULU
the donkey

HI, I'M MELO!

MELO MEANS "THE ONE WHO STANDS FOR GOOD THINGS".

Melo loves to spend time with her animal friends. As they explore and have adventures she learns a lot of wise lessons from Queen Nzinga and her friends.

Use the spaces below to draw or write the names of your friends and what you like best about each one.

If your friends were animals, which animal would each one be?

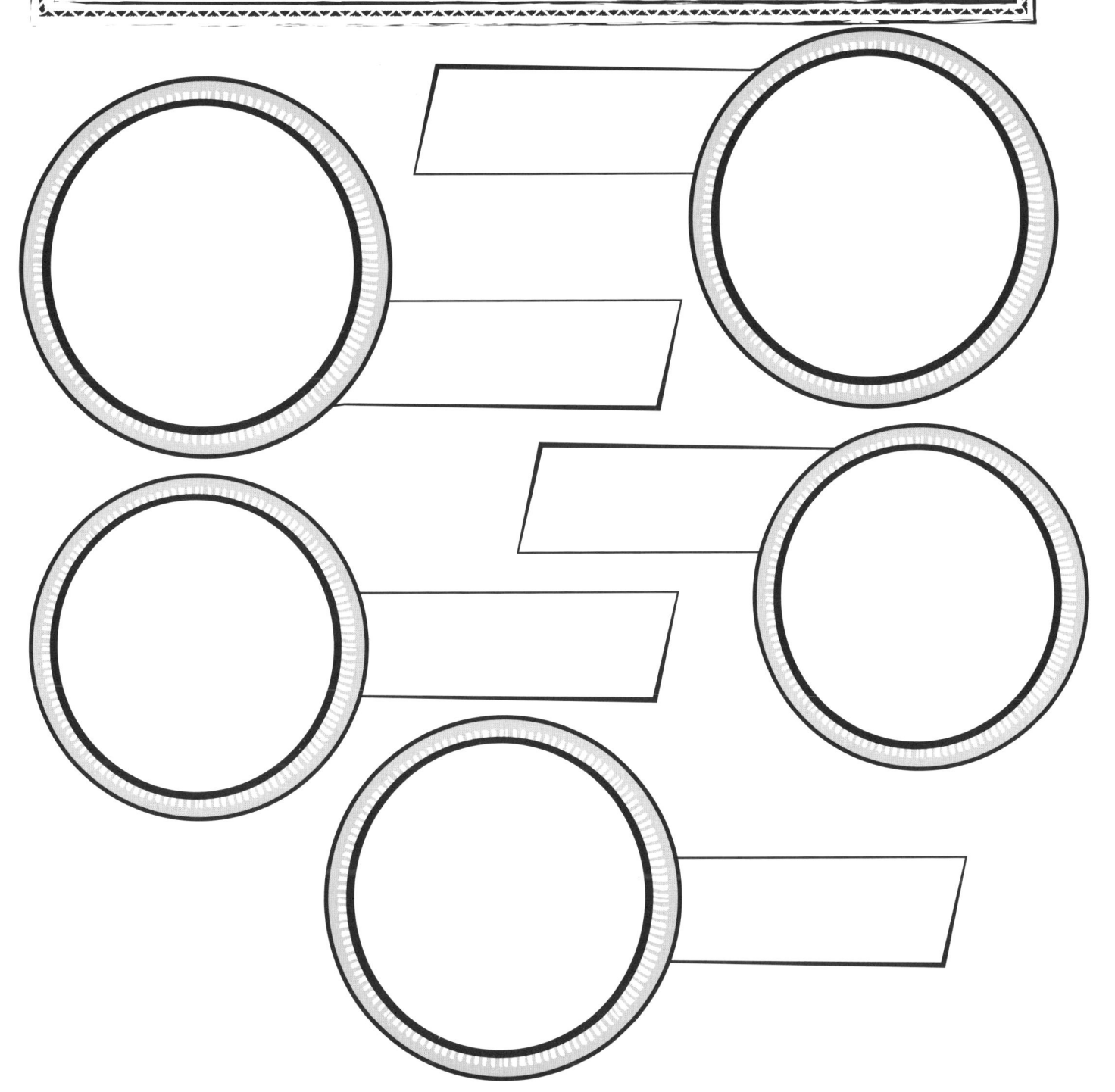

01

GOD IS GOOD!

My favorite Bible verse is ...

Thank You for making me so wonderfully complex!
Your workmanship is marvelous – how well I know it!

PSALM 139:14

What is your favorite animal?

I'm thankful for ...

Write a prayer to thank God for everything
in the wonderful animal kingdom that He created.

How many of QUEEN NZINGA the elephant can you see?

03

"Seek the Kingdom of God above all else, and live righteously, and He will give you everything you need." MATTHEW 6:33

SPOT THE DIFFERENCES

There are 6 differences between the pictures. Can you spot them all?

All things bright and beautiful, all creatures great and small, all things wise and wonderful, the Lord God made them all!

Which object on the right is NOT A MIRROR IMAGE of the object on the left?

05

As a face is reflected in water, so the heart reflects the real person. PROVERBS 27:19

06

HELP QUEEN NZINGA
find her way back to Melo and her friends.

SHARE YOUR PLANS with the **LORD** and you will **SUCCEED.**
Proverbs 16:3

Find and circle these **OBJECTS HIDDEN** in the picture below:

- Apple - Cap - Scarf - Star - Bicycle - Book - Fish - Sleeping bag - Dragonfly - Ball

07

Everything on earth will worship You; they will sing Your praises, shouting Your name in glorious songs. PSALM 66:4

ANIMALS IN THE BIBLE

Join each animal with its description on the right.

- Jesus rode on my back into Jerusalem.
  (MARK 11:1-2)

- A lazy person can learn from me.
  (PROVERBS 6:6-8)

- I was with Daniel in the den.
  (DANIEL 6:21-22)

- I swallowed Jonah.
  (JONAH 1:17)

- Elijah received bread and meat from me.
  (1 KINGS 17:6)

COLOR THE PICTURE

09

"Ask the **animals**, and they will TEACH YOU, or ask the **birds** of the air, and they will TELL YOU. Speak to the **earth**, and it will TEACH YOU, or let the **fish** of the sea TELL YOU. The life of every creature and the BREATH OF ALL PEOPLE are in God's hand."

JOB 12:7-8, 10

MATCH EACH ANIMAL TO ITS FOOTPRINTS

Let us walk in the LIGHT of the LORD.
ISAIAH 2:5

COLORFUL CHAMELEON
Color the picture of Aza the chameleon.

Whatever is good and perfect is a gift coming down to us from God our Father, who created all the lights in the heavens. He never changes. JAMES 1:17

FIND AND CIRCLE
the animals that only eat meat.

> Our Lord, by Your wisdom You made so many things;
> the whole earth is covered with Your living creatures. PSALM 104:24

COLOR WISE NOMKHOSI OWL
according to the number code.

Spend time with the wise & you will become **WISE.**

PROVERBS 13:20

| 1. Brown | 2. Light Brown | 3. Gray | 4. Green |
| 5. Yellow | 6. Red | 7. Blue | 8. Orange |

13

MATCH THE ANIMAL ON THE LEFT WITH ITS SHADOW ON THE RIGHT.

Every wild and tame animal, all reptiles and birds, come praise the LORD! PSALM 148:10

BE BRAVE LIKE A LION

Connect the dots to complete the picture of Tambo the lion and color it in.

BE STRONG and BRAVE.

DEUTERONOMY 31:6

15

16

UNSCRAMBLE THE LETTERS to find the names of 5 animals.
Take the letters that appear in the circled spaces and write them in the spaces below to complete the sentence in the block.

OLW _ _ⓞ

NOMYEK _ⓞ_ _ _ _

LTVUREU _ⓞ_ _ _ _ _

ATENREAT _ _ _ⓞ_ _ _ _

ROTSITEO _ _ _ _ _ⓞ_ _

JESUS _ _ _ _ _ YOU!

HELP MELO AND HER FRIENDS

find their way to the hut.

END

START

Seek God's will in all you do,
and He will show you which path to take. PROVERBS 3:6

17

GOD'S WONDERFUL WORLD

Each number stands for a letter of the alphabet.
Write the correct letter in the blanks
to find the coded words.

___ ___ ___ ___
12   9   15   14

___ ___ ___ ___ ___ ___
13   15   14   11   5   25

___ ___ ___ ___ ___ ___ ___
 7   9   18   1   6   6   5

___ ___ ___ ___ ___ ___ ___ ___ ___
 3   8   1   13   5   12   5   15   14

___ ___ ___   ___ ___ ___   ___ ___ ___ ___ ___ ___
25   15   21   1   18   5   19   16   5   3   9   1   12

A	B	C	D	E	F	G	H	I	J	K	L	M	N	O	P	Q	R	S	T	U	V	W	X	Y	Z
1	2	3	4	5	6	7	8	9	10	11	12	13	14	15	16	17	18	19	20	21	22	23	24	25	26

COLOR THE PICTURE

19

LORD OUR LORD, YOUR NAME IS THE MOST WONDERFUL NAME IN ALL THE EARTH!

PSALM 8:1

JOIN EACH PICTURE

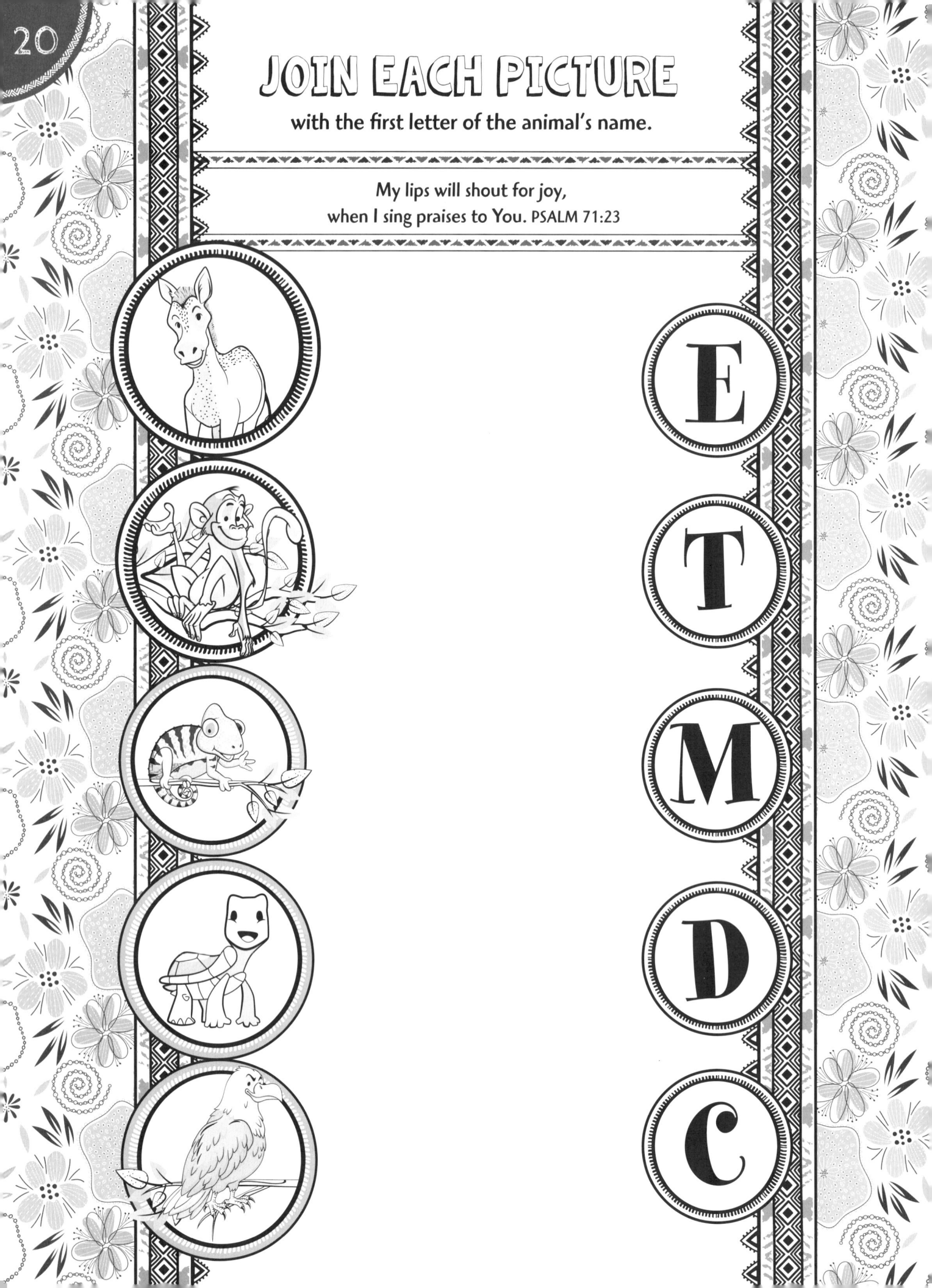

with the first letter of the animal's name.

My lips will shout for joy,
when I sing praises to You. PSALM 71:23

E

T

M

D

C

SPOT THE ODD ONE OUT
in each row of pictures.

Discover for yourself that the Lord is kind. Come to Him for protection, and you will be glad. PSALM 34:8

COLOR THE BIBLE VERSE

"FOR I KNOW THE PLANS I HAVE FOR YOU," SAYS THE LORD

JEREMIAH 29:11

PICTURE SUDOKU

Every row (up, down, right and left) must contain all four pictures - A, B, C, D.

A   B   C   D

"I love all who LOVE Me. Those who search will surely FIND Me."
PROVERBS 8:17

LINE MAZE

Color the path that leads to Melo.

"I am the LORD your God, who teaches you what is good for you and leads you along the paths you should follow."
ISAIAH 48:17

ANIMAL PATTERNS

Which animal is next in the sequence? Fill the correct letter in the space.

A B C D E F G H I

Let every living creature praise the Lord. Shout praises to the Lord! PSALM 150:6

25

DOODLE AND DRAW

Draw leaves on the tree for the giraffe to eat. Add some fruit to the tree.
Draw the sun and sky and some green grass and flowers.

Then God looked over all He had made,
and He saw that it was very good! GENESIS 1:31

HOW MANY EAGLES CAN YOU COUNT?

Those who trust the LORD will find new strength. They will be strong like eagles ... they will walk and run without getting tired. ISAIAH 40:31

27

CONNECT THE DOTS
and color the picture.

GOD MADE THE EARTH AND EVERYTHING IN IT.
PSALM 24:1

SPOT THE DIFFERENCES

Can you spot 6 differences between the two pictures?

There is a time for everything, and a season for every activity under the heavens. ECCLESIASTES 3:1

30

COLOR THE BIBLE VERSE

PHILIPPIANS 4:13

Christ gives me the strength to face anything

SHADOW MATCH

Draw lines from Melo and her friends to their matching shadows.

31

Sing to the Lord with grateful praise. Psalm 147:7

COUNTING MAZE

Help Ganga the monkey find his delicious fruit by following the number maze from 1 to 20.

> The Holy Spirit produces this kind of fruit in our lives: love, joy, peace, patience, kindness, goodness, faithfulness, gentleness, and self-control. GALATIANS 5:22-23

1	2	1	3	4
4	3	2	1	2
2	4	3	5	8

8	7	10	7	5	6	5	6
9	11	12	9	10	7	8	6
10	12	11	10	9	8	10	11
15	13	14	16	20	19	18	20

12	14	18	11	19
17	15	16	19	20
20	18	17	18	16

JOIN EACH LETTER TO THE PICTURE

with the same first letter.

> GOD GIVES food to the wild animals and feeds the young ravens when they cry.
> **Psalm 147:9**

S H Z L B F G

33

How many times can you FIND THE WORD LION in the word search.

> The lions roar for their prey and seek their food from God.
> **PSALM 104:21**

L	L	L						
O	I	L	I	O	N	L		
L	I	O	N	O	O	L	L	
L	I	N	L	N	L	N	I	
L	I	O	N	L	I	I	O	O
I	L	L	I	O	N	O	L	N
O	L	I	O	N	L	N	N	L
N	I	O	O	L	I	O	N	L	I
O	N	L	I	O	N	I	I	O
N	L	I	O	N	L	I	O	N
I	L	N	L	I	I	N	O
O	I	L	I	L	N	O
O	I	O	I	L	L	N	L
N	O	N	O	L	I	O	N
L	N	O	N	L	L	I	O	N
O	N	O	L	I	O	N	I	L	L	I	O	N
L	I	O	L	I	O	N	L	I	O	N	O	O	L	I	O	N
N	O	L	I	O	N	I	L	N	N	N	N

MATCH THE ANIMAL AND ITS TAIL

Our Lord and Ruler, Your name is wonderful everywhere on earth! PSALM 8:9

35

REARRANGE THE LETTERS
to find the names of 6 of Melo's animal friends:

GRAFFEI → _____

HIPOPP → _____

NKEOYM → _____

ABRAZE → _____

LAEHNPET → _____

LAEPEDOR → _____

As iron sharpens iron, friends sharpen the minds of each other.
PROVERB 27:17

COLOR THE ANIMALS that have four legs.

37

"For all the animals of the forest are Mine,
and I own the cattle on a thousand hills.
I know every bird on the mountains,
and all the animals of the field are Mine."

PSALM 50:10-11

COLOR THE BIBLE VERSE

Always be full of joy in the Lord. I say it again — rejoice!

PHILIPPIANS 4:4

COUNT THE STONES

How many stones will Melo find on her way to visit Kiboko the hippo?
Count and number each stone.

A FRIEND LOVES AT ALL TIMES.

PROVERBS 17:17

COLOR THE NUMBER CODE

to reveal the missing word.

For this is how God __ __ __ __ __ the world: He gave His one and only Son, so that everyone who believes in Him will not perish but have eternal life.

JOHN 3:16

1	2	3	4
Blue	Red	Green	Yellow

WORD SEARCH

Find the names of the animals in the word search below.

The LORD is good to all; He has compassion on all He has made. PSALM 145:9

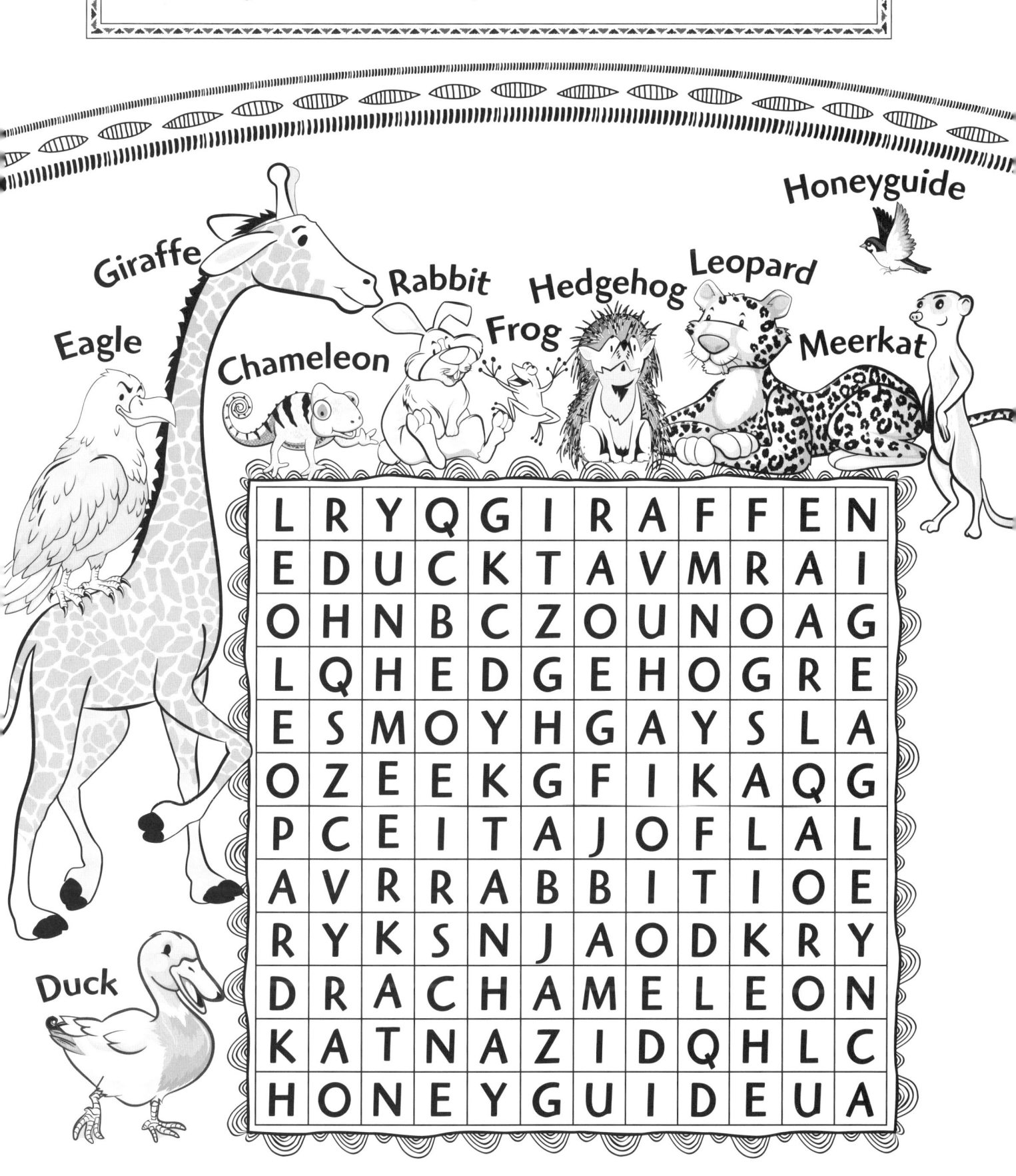

Giraffe · Eagle · Chameleon · Rabbit · Frog · Hedgehog · Leopard · Honeyguide · Meerkat · Duck

L	R	Y	Q	G	I	R	A	F	F	E	N
E	D	U	C	K	T	A	V	M	R	A	I
O	H	N	B	C	Z	O	U	N	O	A	G
L	Q	H	E	D	G	E	H	O	G	R	E
E	S	M	O	Y	H	G	A	Y	S	L	A
O	Z	E	E	K	G	F	I	K	A	Q	G
P	C	E	I	T	A	J	O	F	L	A	L
A	V	R	R	A	B	B	I	T	I	O	E
R	Y	K	S	N	J	A	O	D	K	R	Y
D	R	A	C	H	A	M	E	L	E	O	N
K	A	T	N	A	Z	I	D	Q	H	L	C
H	O	N	E	Y	G	U	I	D	E	U	A

PICTURE SUDOKU

Every row (up, down, left and right) must contain all four pictures - A, B, C, D.

A   B   C   D

A sweet friendship refreshes the soul.
PROVERBS 27:9

FIND THE CORRECT PATH TO THE HEART

Give thanks to the Lord, for He is good! His faithful *love endures forever.*

PSALM 136:1

FILL IN THE MISSING WORDS
to find out who is always ready to help you.

I LOOK UP to the _ _ _ _ _ _

but where does my _ _ _ _ come from?

MY HELP COMES

from the _ _ _ _

who made _ _ _ _ _ _ _

& _ _ _ _ _.

PSALM 121:1-2

hills   Lord
heaven   help   earth

JOIN THE DOTS AND COMPLETE THE PICTURE

of Kiboko the hippo.

Always be joyful. Never stop praying. Be thankful in all circumstances.
1 THESSALONIANS 5:16-18

45

MATCH THE ZEBRA

Which one of the six zebras below match Zenzo the zebra in the rectangle?

For we are God's masterpiece.
He has created us anew in Christ Jesus,
so we can do the good things
He planned for us long ago.
EPHESIANS 2:10

COLOR AND COUNT

47

Color the picture. Can you count how many birds are in the picture?

"Look at the birds of the air: they neither sow nor reap nor gather into barns, and yet your heavenly Father feeds them. Are you not of more value than they?" MATTHEW 6:26

HOW MANY WORDS CAN YOU MAKE WITH HIPPOPOTAMUS

Every word of God proves true. He is a shield to all who come to Him for protection. PROVERBS 30:5

HIPPOPOTAMUS

BLOCK-BY-BLOCK DRAWING

Draw the squirrel block-by-block, using each block as a guideline.

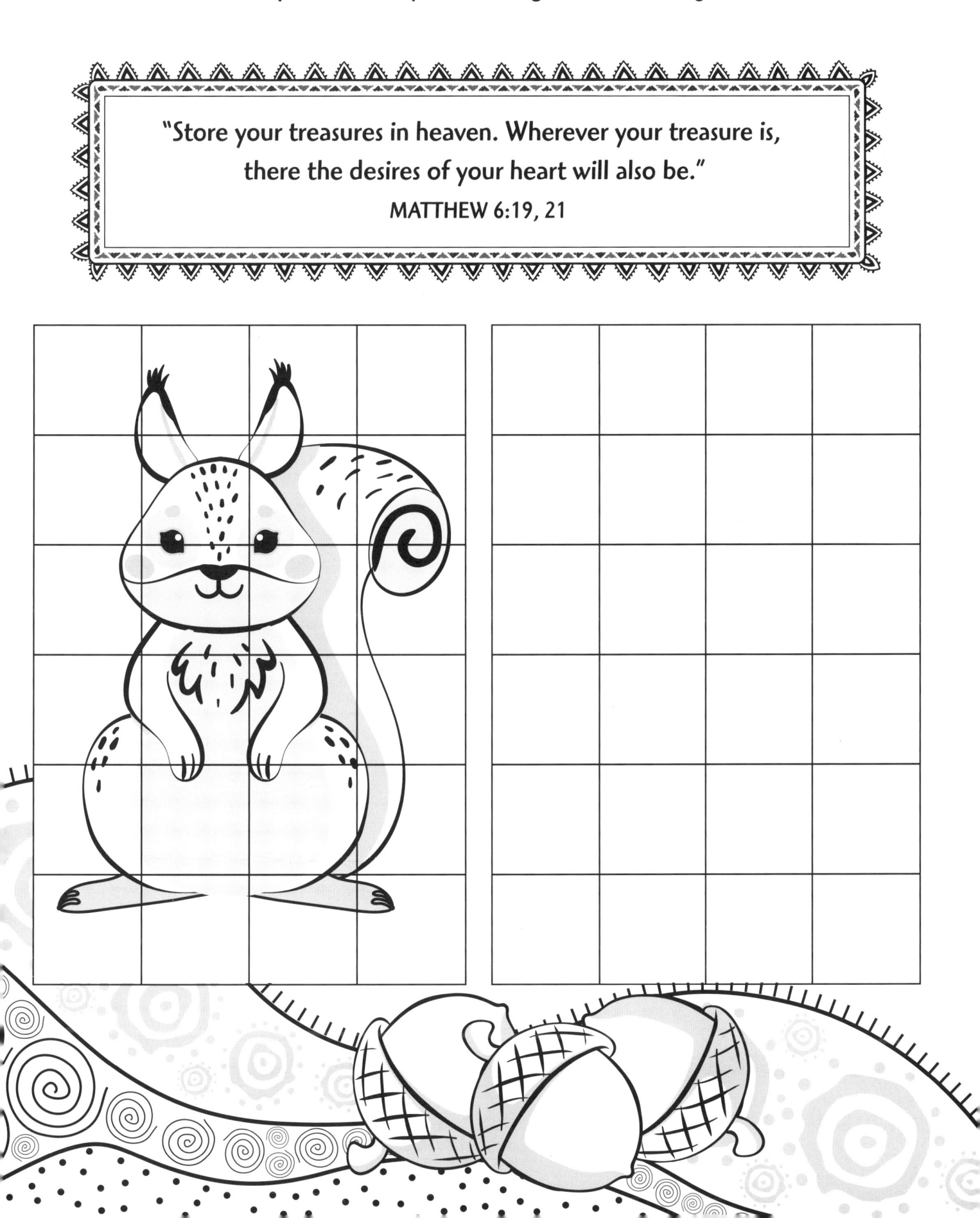

"Store your treasures in heaven. Wherever your treasure is, there the desires of your heart will also be."

MATTHEW 6:19, 21

49

ALPHABET JUMBLE

See if you can spot and color all the letters of the alphabet.
Use the block below to write something that you are thankful to God for.

I am grateful to God for

COLOR THESE CARDS & BOOKMARKS

Cut them out and share them with your friends.

SMILE! JESUS LOVES YOU.

BE BRAVE God is with you.

YOU'RE ONE IN A CHA-MILLION!

I think you are **PAW-SOME!**

A friend loves at all times.
PROVERBS 17:17